Boost!

Reading 3

PEARSON
Longman

Jason Renshaw

Series Editors: Cecilia Petersen and Mayumi Tabuchi

Published by
Pearson Longman Asia ELT
20/F Cornwall House
Taikoo Place
979 King's Road
Quarry Bay
Hong Kong

fax: +852 2856 9578
email: pearsonlongman@pearsoned.com.hk
www.longman.com

and Associated Companies throughout the world.

First published 2007
Reprinted 2007 (twice)

Produced by Pearson Education Asia Limited, Hong Kong
GCC/03

ISBN-13: 978-962-00-5871-4
ISBN-10: 962-00-5871-2

Publisher: Simon Campbell
Project Editor: Howard Cheung
Editor: Jessica Balde
Designers: Junko Funaki, Jack Wong
Illustrator: Balic Choy
Audio Production: David Pope and Sky Productions

For permission to use copyrighted images, we would like to thank © Bob Rowan; Progressive Image/Corbis (pp. 4 RT and 10 T), © Robbie Jack/Corbis (pp. 4 RC and 10 C), © B. Bird/zefa/Corbis (pp. 4 RB and 10 B), © H. Schmid/zefa/Corbis (p. 16 L), © Martyn Goddard/Corbis (p. 16 R), © Brynner Victoria/Corbis Sygma (pp. 5 B and 17), © NASA Jet Propulsion Laboratory (pp. 19, 20 B and 27), © Steve Lee (University of Colorado); Jim Bell (Cornell University); Mike Wolff (Space Science Institute); NASA (p. 20 T), © 1989 Roger Ressmeyer/NASA/Corbis (p. 20 C), © The International Astronomical Union/Martin Kornmesser (p. 23) © Dr. R. Albrecht, ESA/ESO Space Telescope European Coordinating Facility; NASA (p. 24), © Larry Williams/Corbis (p. 29 Bkgd), © George Shelley/Corbis (p. 29 T), Chris Stowers © Dorling Kindersley (p. 33 Bkgd), © Atlantide Phototravel/Corbis (p. 34 T, C), © Daniel Lavabre (p. 37 T, B), © Douglas Kirkland/Corbis (p. 39 C), © S. Carmona/Corbis (p. 40 T), © Duomo/Corbis (p. 40 B), © Ilya Pitalev/ITAR-TASS/Corbis (pp. 43 and 44 B), © Vitaly Belousov/ITAR-TASS/Corbis (p. 44 T), © Troy Wayrynen/NewSport/Corbis (p. 46), © Connie Ricca/Corbis (p. 53 R Bkgd), © Simon Marcus/Corbis (p. 53 L), © LWA-Stephen Welstead/Corbis (p. 59), © Envision/Corbis (p. 64 TT, CC, BT, BB), © Y.Bagros/photocuisine/Corbis (p. 64 TC, BC), © J.Riou/photocuisine/Corbis (p. 64 TB), © Paul Anton/zefa/Corbis (p. 64 CT) and © Lew Robertson/Corbis (p. 64 CB).

Acknowledgements
These reading books are dedicated to my beloved wife, Yeona. Without her patience, support and encouragement, the Boost! series would not have been possible for me to write. Thank you also to the Korean teachers at Jasaeng JS English in Changwon, South Korea, who have been my partners in finding better ways to teach reading skills to young and teenage learners.
Jason Renshaw

The Publishers would also like to thank the following teachers for their suggestions and comments on this course:
Tara Cameron, Rosanne Cerello, Nancy Chan, Chang Li Ping, Joy Chao, Jessie Chen, Josephine Chen, Chiang Ying-hsueh, Claire Cho, Cindy Chuang, Linda Chuang, Chueh Shiu-wen, Mark de Boer, Mieko Hayashida, Diana Ho, Lulu Hsu, Eunice Jung, Hye Ri Kim, Jake Kimball, Josie Lai, Carol Lee, Elaine Lee, Melody Lee, Peggy Li, Esther Lim, Moon Jeong Lim, Jasmin Lin, Martin Lin, Catherine Littlehale Oki, Linda Liu, Tammy Liu, Goldie Luk, Ma Li-ling, Chizuko Matsushita, Geordie McGarty, Yasuyo Mito, Eunice Izumi Miyashita, Mari Nakamura, Yannick O'Neill, Coco Pan, Hannah Park, Karen Peng, Zanne Schultz, Kaj Schwermer, Mi Yeon Shin, Giant Shu, Dean Stafford, Hyunju Suh, Tan Yung-hui, Devon Thagard, John and Charlie van Goch, Annie Wang, Wang Shu-ling, Wu Lien-chun, Sabrina Wu, Yeh Shihfen, Tom Yeh, Laura Yoshida and Yunji Yun.

Welcome to

The **Boost!** Skills Series is the definitive and comprehensive four-level series of skills books for junior EFL learners. The series has been developed around age-appropriate, cross-curricular topics that develop students' critical thinking and examination techniques. It follows an integrated skills approach with each of the skills brought together at the end of each unit.

The twelve core units in **Boost! Reading 3** follow a clear and transparent structure to make teaching and learning easy and fun. The reading skills build and progress across the four levels of **Boost! Reading** and are correlated to the next generation of tests of English.

You will find the following in **Boost! Reading 3**:

- Age-appropriate and cross-curricular content-based passages
- A wide variety of text types (academic readings, reports, emails, newspaper articles, etc.)
- Units paired by theme, with a review unit for each pair

Unit Topic

Each unit has a cross-curricular and age-appropriate topic.

Students will

- find the topic directly relates to their own lives and study.
- be engaged and motivated to learn.

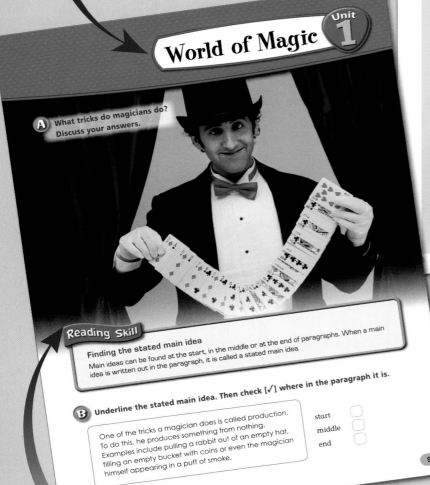

Unit **1**
World of Magic

A What tricks do magicians do? Discuss your answers.

Reading Skill

Finding the stated main idea

Main ideas can be found at the start, in the middle or at the end of paragraphs. When a main idea is written out in the paragraph, it is called a stated main idea.

B Underline the stated main idea. Then check [✓] where in the paragraph it is.

One of the tricks a magician does is called production. To do this, he produces something from nothing. Examples include pulling a rabbit out of an empty hat, filling an empty bucket with coins or even the magician himself appearing in a puff of smoke.

start ☐
middle ☐
end ☐

C ▶ 2 Read the passage.

It's magic!

Magicians perform magic tricks to show that something impossible has happened. There are many kinds of magic tricks.

One kind of magic trick is called production. To do this, a magician produces something from nothing. Examples include pulling a rabbit out of an empty hat, filling an empty bucket with coins or even the magician himself appearing in a puff of smoke.

A magician is holding a coin. He might snap his fingers and the coin suddenly disappears. This trick is an example of the vanish, which is the opposite of production. The vanish is a kind of magic trick in which things disappear. After putting a bird in a cage and then covering the cage with cloth, the magician waves his wand and pulls away the cloth. The bird has vanished.

Perhaps a rope is cut in half with a knife. The magician does something special and suddenly the rope is one complete piece again. Or after tearing a newspaper into pieces, the magician rubs the pieces together and the newspaper becomes whole again. These tricks restore things to the way they were before. Restoration is another common type of magic trick.

9

Reading

A graded, content-based reading passage, with supporting audio, sets up the main skill practice.

Students will

- find the reading passage stimulating with topics geared to their age level.
- be exposed to a variety of text types—from academic to real-world passages.
- be able to answer comprehension questions to aid understanding.

Reading Skill

A very simple introduction of the targeted unit skill is followed by a skill discovery activity.

Students will

- be introduced to the reading skill in a clear and understandable way.
- discover the reading skill for themselves without the need for long explanations.

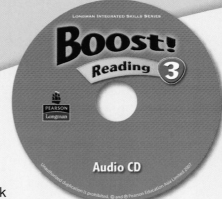

LONGMAN INTEGRATED SKILLS SERIES

Boost! Reading **3**

PEARSON Longman

Audio CD

Audio CD

The CD at the back of the book provides audio support for all reading passages plus the audio for the Integration listening tasks.

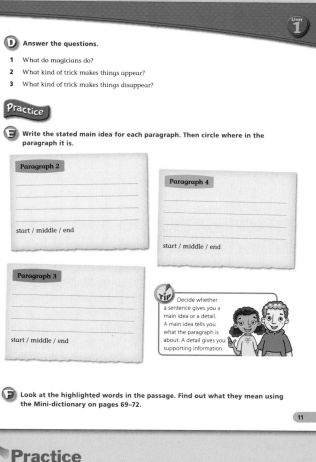

D Answer the questions.

1　What do magicians do?

2　What kind of trick makes things appear?

3　What kind of trick makes things disappear?

Practice

E Write the stated main idea for each paragraph. Then circle where in the paragraph it is.

Paragraph 2

_____
_____
_____
_____

start / middle / end

Paragraph 4

_____
_____
_____
_____

start / middle / end

Paragraph 3

_____
_____
_____
_____

start / middle / end

> **Tip** Decide whether a sentence gives you a main idea or a detail. A main idea tells you what the paragraph is about. A detail gives you supporting information.

F Look at the highlighted words in the passage. Find out what they mean using the Mini-dictionary on pages 69–72.

11

Integration

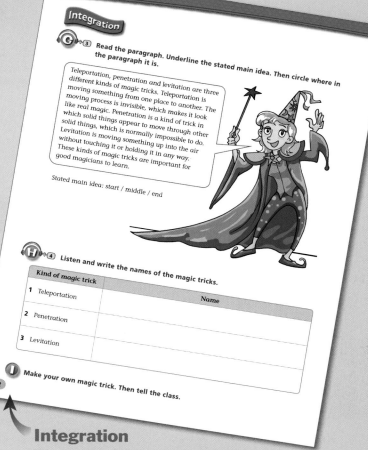

G 3 Read the paragraph. Underline the stated main idea. Then circle where in the paragraph it is.

Teleportation, penetration and levitation are three different kinds of magic tricks. Teleportation is moving something from one place to another. The moving process is invisible, which makes it look like real magic. Penetration is a kind of trick in which solid things appear to move through other solid things, which is normally impossible to do. Levitation is moving something up into the air without touching it or holding it in any way. These kinds of magic tricks are important for good magicians to learn.

Stated main idea: start / middle / end

H 4 Listen and write the names of the magic tricks.

Kind of magic trick	Name
1 Teleportation	
2 Penetration	
3 Levitation	

I Make your own magic trick. Then tell the class.

12

Practice

A skill practice task is followed by an independent vocabulary-building activity using the Mini-dictionary.

Students will

- be able to apply the reading skill to the passage through meaningful practice.
- develop their vocabulary by learning words in context.

Integration

The reading skill is combined with listening, writing or speaking tasks.

Students will

- learn to use a reading passage to springboard into productive activities.
- develop the language skills needed for the next generation of integrated tests of English.

Review

After every two core units there is a review which consolidates the reading skills already studied.

Students will

- be able to see their progress in using reading skills.
- learn to apply different reading skills to the same passage.

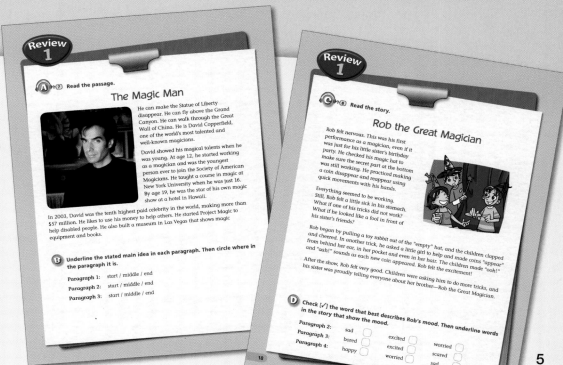

Review 1

A 7 Read the passage.

The Magic Man

He can make the Statue of Liberty disappear. He can fly above the Grand Canyon. He can walk through the Great Wall of China. He is David Copperfield, one of the world's most talented and well-known magicians.

David showed his magical talents when he was young. At age 12, he started working as a magician and was the youngest person ever to join the Society of American Magicians. He taught a course in magic at New York University when he was just 16. By age 19, he was the star of his own magic show at a hotel in Hawaii.

In 2003, David was the tenth highest paid celebrity in the world, making more than $57 million. He likes to use his money to help others. He started Project Magic to help disabled people. He also built a museum in Las Vegas that shows magic equipment and books.

B Underline the stated main idea in each paragraph. Then circle where in the paragraph it is.

Paragraph 1:　start / middle / end

Paragraph 2:　start / middle / end

Paragraph 3:　start / middle / end

18

Review 1

C 8 Read the story.

Rob the Great Magician

Rob felt nervous. This was his first performance as a magician, even if it was just for his little sister's birthday party. He checked his magic hat to make sure the secret part at the bottom was still working. He practiced making a coin disappear and reappear using quick movements with his hands.

Everything seemed to be working. Still, Rob felt a little sick in his stomach. What if one of his tricks did not work? What if he looked like a fool in front of his sister's friends?

Rob began by pulling a toy rabbit out of the "empty" hat, and the children clapped and cheered. In another trick, he asked a little girl to help and made coins "appear" from behind her ear, in her pocket and even in her hair. The children made "ooh!" and "aah!" sounds as each new coin appeared. Rob felt the excitement!

After the show, Rob felt very good. Children were asking him to do more tricks, and his sister was proudly telling everyone about her brother—Rob the Great Magician.

D Check [✓] the word that best describes Rob's mood. Then underline words in the story that show the mood.

Paragraph 2:　sad ☐　excited ☐　worried ☐
Paragraph 3:　bored ☐　excited ☐　scared ☐
Paragraph 4:　happy ☐　worried ☐　sad ☐

5

Contents

Evaluation

	Successful with the skill	Needs to review the skill	Comments
Unit 1 Finding the stated main idea			
Unit 2 Identifying moods			
Unit 3 Cross-scanning for details			
Unit 4 Finding information from tables			
Unit 5 Understanding settings			
Unit 6 Understanding brochures			
Unit 7 Understanding summaries			
Unit 8 Identifying character			
Unit 9 Understanding paragraph development			
Unit 10 Understanding signs			
Unit 11 Finding information from graphs			
Unit 12 Understanding menus			

A What tricks do magicians do? Discuss your answers.

Reading Skill

Finding the stated main idea

Main ideas can be found at the start, in the middle or at the end of paragraphs. When a main idea is written out in the paragraph, it is called a stated main idea.

B Underline the stated main idea. Then check [✓] where in the paragraph it is.

One of the tricks a magician does is called production. To do this, he produces something from nothing. Examples include pulling a rabbit out of an empty hat, filling an empty bucket with coins or even the magician himself appearing in a puff of smoke.

start ☐
middle ✓
end ☐

It's magic!

Magicians perform magic tricks to show that something impossible has happened. There are many kinds of magic tricks.

One kind of magic trick is called production. To do this, a magician produces something from nothing. Examples include pulling a rabbit out of an empty hat, filling an empty bucket with coins or even the magician himself appearing in a puff of smoke.

A magician is holding a coin. He might snap his fingers and the coin suddenly disappears. This trick is an example of the vanish, which is the opposite of production. The vanish is a kind of magic trick in which things disappear. After putting a bird in a cage and then covering the cage with cloth, the magician waves his wand and pulls away the cloth. The bird has vanished.

Perhaps a rope is cut in half with a knife. The magician does something special and suddenly the rope is one complete piece again. Or after tearing a newspaper into pieces, the magician rubs the pieces together and the newspaper becomes whole again. These tricks restore things to the way they were before. Restoration is another common type of magic trick.

D Answer the questions.

1 What do magicians do?

2 What kind of trick makes things appear?

3 What kind of trick makes things disappear?

E Write the stated main idea for each paragraph. Then circle where in the paragraph it is.

Paragraph 2 =1

_____

_____

_____

_____

start / middle / end

Paragraph 4 =2

_____

_____

_____

_____

start / middle / end

Paragraph 3 =3

_____

_____

_____

_____

start / middle / end

TIP Decide whether a sentence gives you a main idea or a detail. A main idea tells you what the paragraph is about. A detail gives you supporting information.

F Look at the highlighted words in the passage. Find out what they mean using the Mini-dictionary on pages 69–72.

G 🎧 3 **Read the paragraph. Underline the stated main idea. Then circle where in the paragraph it is.**

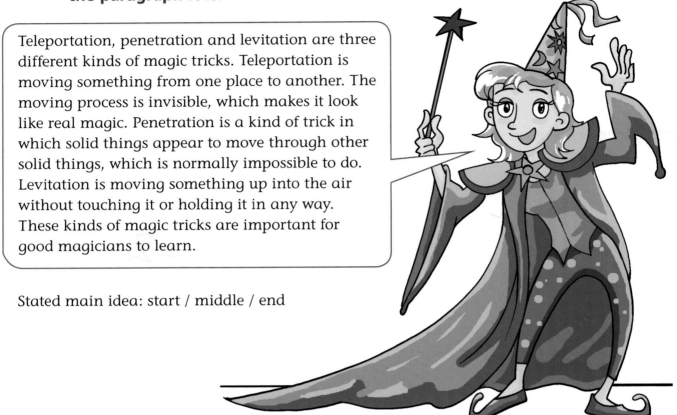

Teleportation, penetration and levitation are three different kinds of magic tricks. Teleportation is moving something from one place to another. The moving process is invisible, which makes it look like real magic. Penetration is a kind of trick in which solid things appear to move through other solid things, which is normally impossible to do. Levitation is moving something up into the air without touching it or holding it in any way. These kinds of magic tricks are important for good magicians to learn.

Stated main idea: start / middle / end

H 🎧 4 **Listen and write the names of the magic tricks.**

Kind of magic trick	Name
1 Teleportation	
2 Penetration	
3 Levitation	

I **Make your own magic trick. Then tell the class.**

(A) **Why are magic shows popular?**
Discuss your answers.

Reading Skill

Identifying moods

Mood is the atmosphere or feeling in a situation. Things you can see, hear or feel create the mood. Writers create moods in their stories by giving detailed descriptions.

(B) **Check [✓] the moods you can identify.**

> Suddenly the stage began to fill up with green smoke. The audience became silent and everybody stared. With a flash of multicolored lights, Peter appeared right in the middle of the stage. The audience gasped.

happy ☐
exciting ☐
boring ☐
sad ☐
scary ☐

The Amazing Peter Twinklehands

Julie was in the theater, sitting with her dad. The stage in front of her was dark and silent. Behind her, she could hear the rest of the audience chattering excitedly. What amazing magic would Peter Twinklehands perform tonight? Would he do his flying motorcycle trick?

Suddenly the stage began to fill up with green smoke. The audience became silent and everybody stared. With a flash of multicolored lights, Peter appeared right in the middle of the stage. The audience gasped.

"Good evening, my dear people," said Peter. His voice was soft but it sounded powerful. "I have many wonderful acts to perform for you tonight, so I should get started right away."

Peter suddenly leaned forward and pointed straight at Julie, his eyes wide and scary.

"You!" he said. "Do you want me to make your dad disappear?" He clapped his hands together and the whole theater echoed loudly.

Julie was scared. She turned to look at her dad, but he was gone! She panicked and wanted to cry. Where was her dad? She turned back to Peter to demand that he return her dad, but Peter was already getting ready for his next trick. "Bring out my motorcycle!" he called.

For the next couple of minutes, Julie watched the magic show, numb and scared. Suddenly a voice behind her said, "I bought you some popcorn." It was her dad!

From the stage, Peter looked down at her and winked.

D **Answer the questions.**

1 How did the audience feel before the show started?

2 What did the audience do when Peter Twinklehands appeared?

3 Did Peter Twinklehands really make Julie's dad disappear? How do you know?

E **Write a sentence from the story that shows mood.**

1 scary

The stage in front of her
was dark and silent.

3 sad

2 exciting

4 happy

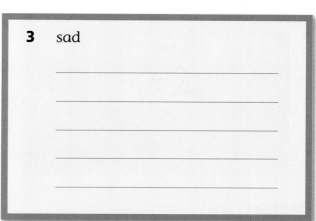

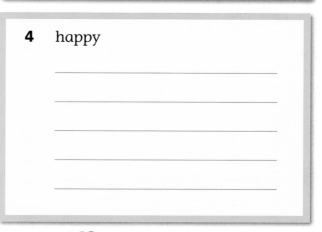

TIP Look for sentences that describe how people react or feel.

F **Look at the highlighted words in the story. Find out what they mean using the Mini-dictionary on pages 69–72.**

Integration

G 🎧6 **Read the sentences. Then identify the mood.**

1   The weather was bright and sunny, and the air smelled so fresh.   _____

2   The girl walked slowly and heavily, looking down at her feet.   _____

3   His eyes were shining, and his face was full of excitement.   _____

4   She heard a noise behind her in the darkness. Her skin felt cold.   _____

H **Identify the mood in each photo. Then write a sentence that describes the mood.**

1

Mood: _____

Sentence: _____

_____

_____

2

Mood: _____

Sentence: _____

_____

_____

I **Write a sentence that describes your mood today. Then tell the class.**

Mood: _____

Sentence: _____

_____

_____

 Read the passage.

The Magic Man

He can make the Statue of Liberty disappear. He can fly above the Grand Canyon. He can walk through the Great Wall of China. He is David Copperfield, one of the world's most talented and well-known magicians.

David showed his magical talents when he was young. At age 12, he started working as a magician and was the youngest person ever to join the Society of American Magicians. He taught a course in magic at New York University when he was just 16. By age 19, he was the star of his own magic show at a hotel in Hawaii.

In 2003, David was the tenth highest paid celebrity in the world, making more than $57 million. He likes to use his money to help others. He started Project Magic to help disabled people. He also built a museum in Las Vegas that shows magic equipment and books.

B **Underline the stated main idea in each paragraph. Then circle where in the paragraph it is.**

Paragraph 1:   start / middle / end

Paragraph 2:   start / middle / end

Paragraph 3:   start / middle / end

 **Read the story.**

Rob the Great Magician

Rob felt nervous. This was his first performance as a magician, even if it was just for his little sister's birthday party. He checked his magic hat to make sure the secret part at the bottom was still working. He practiced making a coin disappear and reappear using quick movements with his hands.

Everything seemed to be working. Still, Rob felt a little sick in his stomach. What if one of his tricks did not work? What if he looked like a fool in front of his sister's friends?

Rob began by pulling a toy rabbit out of the "empty" hat, and the children clapped and cheered. In another trick, he asked a little girl to help and made coins "appear" from behind her ear, in her pocket and even in her hair. The children made "ooh!" and "aah!" sounds as each new coin appeared. Rob felt the excitement!

After the show, Rob felt very good. Children were asking him to do more tricks, and his sister was proudly telling everyone about her brother—Rob the Great Magician.

D **Check [✓] the word that best describes Rob's mood. Then underline words in the story that show the mood.**

Paragraph 2:	sad ☐	excited ☐	worried ☐
Paragraph 3:	bored ☐	excited ☐	scared ☐
Paragraph 4:	happy ☐	worried ☐	sad ☐

Mission to Mars

A What do you know about the planet Mars? Discuss your answers.

Reading Skill

Cross-scanning for details

Cross-scanning means looking from one side of a paragraph to another, instead of reading every word. It is an easier way of finding details.

B Read the questions. Then cross-scan the paragraph by following the lines. You have 10 seconds to find and circle the answers.

a Which agency sent the Viking robots to Mars?

b When was the Viking mission sent to Mars?

c What did the Viking robots measure?

d What did the Viking robot photograph?

> ① One of the first successful missions ② to Mars took place in 1976. In this mission, two Viking robots were sent by NASA, the U.S. space agency. The Viking robots measured the daily temperature and one of them took a photograph of a hill that is ③ now known as the "face on Mars." ④

 Read the passage.

Looking for Life on Mars

Scientists have long been interested in the planet Mars. It is one of the planets nearest to Earth and it is probably the most similar, too. Some scientists even think that humans can live on Mars in the future.

Over the past 40 years there have been many attempts to visit Mars to get information. Of the 37 attempts to reach Mars, 19 ended in disaster. Only six missions were able to send information back to Earth.

One of the first successful missions took place in 1976. In this mission, two Viking robots were sent to Mars by NASA, the U.S. space agency. The Viking robots measured the daily temperature and one of them took a photograph of a hill that is now known as the "face on Mars."

The most recent successful missions used rovers—special robots that can move around the surface of the planet. The rovers found proof that there was once a lot of water on Mars. This made scientists excited about the chance to show that life does (or did) exist on Mars.

The NASA rovers are still in good condition and continue to explore the surface of Mars.

D Answer the questions.

1 Why are scientists interested in Mars?

2 How many attempts have there been to reach Mars?

3 What are rovers?

Practice

E Cross-scan the paragraphs in the passage. You have 2 minutes to find and write the answers.

1 How many missions to Mars ended in disaster? _19._____

2 What were the robots sent to Mars in 1976 called? _____

3 What do scientists think humans can do on Mars in the future? _____

4 How many missions were able to send information back to Earth? _____

5 How long have scientists been trying to visit Mars? _____

6 What can rovers do? _____

_____

7 What did the rovers find proof of on Mars? _____

8 What do the rovers continue to do now? _____

9 What is the name of the U.S. space agency? _____

10 Why were scientists excited about finding water on Mars? _____

_____

TIP Underline the key words in each question and think about them as you cross-scan each paragraph.

F Look at the highlighted words in the passage. Find out what they mean using the Mini-dictionary on pages 69–72.

 G (10) **Should we continue to explore space? Cross-scan the dialogue and underline the reasons.**

Yes, we should continue to explore space. There's still a lot that we don't know about other planets and one day we might find other forms of life. Also, maybe in the future we'll need another planet to live on, so we should continue looking.

No, exploring space costs a lot of money. Also, we still have many problems on our own planet and should work on those first. For example, we can try to find cures for diseases and we should give food to the poor. Those are more important than exploring space.

H **Write what you and three classmates think about exploring space. Then tell the class.**

	Name	Yes	No	Reason
1	Me			
2				
3				
4				

The New Solar System

A **What do you know about the planets that circle the Sun? Discuss your answers.**

Mercury Venus Earth Mars Jupiter Saturn Uranus Neptune

—— Planets

Ceres

Pluto 2003 UB$_{313}$

—— Dwarf Planets

Reading Skill

Finding information from tables

Some information is best shown in tables than in paragraphs. Tables allow you to easily read and compare information.

B **Complete the table using the information in the passage.**

The planet Earth is 12,756 kilometers in diameter and 150 million kilometers from the Sun. It has an average temperature of 15 degrees Celsius. A year has 365 days and one day is 24 hours long.

Saturn, on the other hand, is 120,536 kilometers in diameter and 1,434 million kilometers from the Sun. It has an average surface temperature of −140 degrees Celsius. A year has 10,747 days and one day is about 10 hours and 42 minutes long.

Planet	Diameter (km)	Distance from the Sun (million km)	Average Temperature (°C)	Length of a Year (days)	Length of a Day (hrs. mins.)
Earth					
Saturn					

 **Read the article.**

www.astroinfo.com/news/story_G25L

Pluto is out!

For more than 76 years, we were told that there were nine planets circling the Sun, with Pluto being the last and most distant one. All that changed on August 24, 2006, when the world's astronomers decided that Pluto was no longer a planet. Now our solar system only has eight planets, not nine.

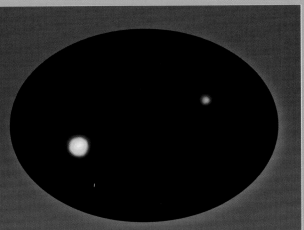

Pluto and its moon, Charon

Scientists have long been arguing about whether or not Pluto is really a planet. Questions about Pluto increased with the discovery of 2003 UB313, an icy object very far from the Sun. But scientists were also not sure if 2003 UB313, now formally known as Eris, should be called a planet.

Eventually, scientists decided that for an object to be classified as a planet, it must meet three criteria:
1 It must circle the Sun.
2 It must be large and round.
3 Its orbit must be free of other objects.

Both Pluto and Eris circle the Sun and are round. But their orbits are strange and are shared with other objects. For those reasons, they cannot be called planets. Instead, they are now called "dwarf planets."

Another object that was classified as a dwarf planet is Ceres, a huge round asteroid between Mars and Jupiter. Scientists expect to announce more dwarf planets in the future.

Dwarf Planet	Diameter (km)	Distance from the Sun (million km)	Average Temperature (°C)	Length of a Year (days)	Length of a Day (hours)
Pluto	2,390	5,870	−225	90,588	153
Eris	3,000	18,000	−300	203,550	8
Ceres	975	413	−106	1,680	9

D Answer the questions.

1 When did scientists decide that Pluto was no longer a planet?

2 What is Pluto now classified as?

3 What is 2003 UB313 formally known as?

Practice

E Look at the table and write the answers.

1 Which dwarf planet has the largest diameter? _____

2 Which dwarf planet has the smallest diameter? _____

3 Which dwarf planet is the warmest? _____

4 Which dwarf planet is the coldest? _____

5 Which dwarf planet has the shortest year? _____

6 Which dwarf planet has the longest year? _____

7 Which dwarf planet has the shortest day? _____

8 Which dwarf planet has the longest day? _____

9 How many days are there in a year on Pluto? _____

10 Which dwarf planet is the closest to the Sun? _____

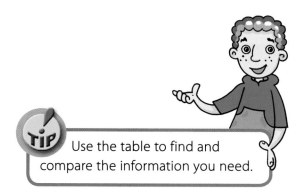

TIP Use the table to find and compare the information you need.

F Look at the highlighted words in the article. Find out what they mean using the Mini-dictionary on pages 69–72.

Integration

G 🎧 (12) **Read the paragraph. Then write the missing information in the table.**

Mercury is the closest planet to the Sun, with a distance of 58 million kilometers. It has a surface temperature of 427 degrees Celsius during the day and –173 degrees Celsius at night. Venus is between Mercury and Earth. A year on Venus is 225 days long and each day lasts for 2,802 hours. Mars is 6,794 kilometers in diameter and is 228 million kilometers from the Sun. A day lasts for 24 hours and 42 minutes.

Planet	Diameter (km)	Distance from the Sun (million km)	Average Temperature (°C)	Length of a Year (days)	Length of a Day (hrs. mins.)
Mercury	4,879		(day) -173 (night)	88	4,222 hrs. 36 mins.
	12,104	108	464		2,802 hrs.
Earth	12,756	150	15	365	24 hrs.
Mars		228	–65	687	
Jupiter		779		4,331	9 hrs. 54 mins.
Saturn	120,536	1,434	–140	10,747	10 hrs. 42 mins.
Uranus	51,118		–195	30,589	
Neptune	49,528	4,495	–200	59,800	16 hrs. 6 mins.

H 🎧 (13) **Listen and complete the table.**

I **Write statements based on the information above. Then tell the class.**

1 Jupiter is the biggest planet in the solar system.

2 _____

3 _____

 Read the passage.

Would life on Mars be better?

Problems on our own planet Earth make a lot of people think that we may need to find a new planet to live on. Of the planets in the solar system, Mars is the most popular choice. It is very similar to Earth, which is why life on Mars might be easier than on other planets.

The Martian and Earth days are almost the same—a day on Mars is about 24 hours. Mars and Earth have about the same land surface area. Both have an atmosphere and water. Mars also has seasons, just like Earth. These similarities mean that life on Mars for humans could be possible—it could be close to the life humans have on Earth.

However, the differences between Mars and Earth make living on Mars challenging. There are 687 days in each Martian year and each season would be nearly twice as long as an Earth season. Even though Mars has an atmosphere, it is very thin and is mainly carbon dioxide—there is not enough oxygen for humans to breathe! There is little water on Mars and it could be very hard to find. Also, it is very cold on Mars and gravity is weaker.

	Earth	Mars
Diameter	12,756 km	6,794 km
Land Surface Area	149 million km²	145 million km²
Distance from the Sun	150 million km	228 million km
Average Temperature	15°C	−65°C
Length of a Year	365 days	687 days
Length of a Day	24 hrs.	24 hrs. 42 mins.

B Underline the stated main idea in each paragraph. Then circle where in the paragraph it is.

Paragraph 1:   start / middle / end

Paragraph 2:   start / middle / end

Paragraph 3:   start / middle / end

C Cross-scan the paragraphs in the passage and write the answers.

1   How are Martian and Earth seasons different?

_____

2   Is the Martian atmosphere thick or thin?

_____

3   What does Earth have that Mars does not have?

_____

4   What do the differences between Mars and Earth mean?

_____

D Look at the table and write the answers.

1   Which planet has a larger diameter?   _____

2   Which planet is farther from the Sun?   _____

3   Which planet is colder?   _____

4   Is the length of a year on Mars and Earth similar or different?   _____

5   Is the length of a day on Mars and Earth similar or different?   _____

A What is exciting about traveling around the world? Discuss your answers.

Reading Skill

Understanding settings

Setting is the time, place and situation in a passage. Knowing the setting helps you identify things that happened in the past, are real in the present or possible in the future.

B Circle the correct setting.

1

The Bering Strait is the sea that separates Alaska from Siberia. The strait is narrow—it is only about 85 km wide. Winters in the strait are long and dark, with the temperature going down as low as –50 degrees Celsius.

past / present / future

2

A bridge connecting Asia and the Americas would be very special. People would be able to travel easily from one side of the world to the other. Trade would increase, and people could learn about other cultures more easily. For these reasons, this bridge would be called the Intercontinental Peace Bridge.

past / present / future

 Read the passage.

Bridge to Tomorrow

The Bering Strait is the sea that separates Alaska from Siberia. The strait is narrow—it is only about 85 km wide. Winters in the strait are long and dark, with the temperature going down as low as –50 degrees Celsius.

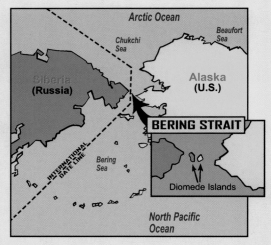

In the middle of the strait are two islands known as the Diomede Islands. The International Date Line runs between the Diomede Islands. This means that from "today" on Little Diomede (on the Alaskan side) you can look across at "tomorrow" on Big Diomede (on the Siberian side). This is also the line that separates the Americas from Asia. Thousands of years ago, these two continents were connected. Lower sea levels during the Ice Age showed a huge land that joined them. People then crossed over from Asia to live all over the Americas.

People are now saying that it is time to connect the continents again. To do this, a huge bridge would need to be built. Of course, it would not be easy. The bridge would take a long time to build and cost billions of dollars. It would need to be strong to withstand icebergs and winter winds. Also, it would probably only be usable during the summer months.

But the bridge would be very special. People would be able to travel easily from one side of the world to the other. Trade would increase, and people could learn about other cultures more easily. For these reasons, this bridge would be called the Intercontinental Peace Bridge.

30

D **Answer the questions.**

1 What does the Bering Strait separate?

2 How wide is the Bering Strait?

3 Why can you see tomorrow from Little Diomede?

E **Check [✓] the statements that show *Past*, *Present* or *Future*.**

		Past	Present	Future
1	A bridge connecting Alaska and Siberia would take a long time to build.			
2	The Bering Strait is the sea that separates Alaska and Siberia.			
3	Thousands of years ago, Asia and the Americas were connected.			
4	People would be able to travel easily from one side of the world to the other.			
5	People crossed over from Asia to live all over the Americas.			
6	People could learn about other cultures more easily.			
7	From "today" on Little Diomede, you can look across at "tomorrow" on Big Diomede.			
8	Lower sea levels during the Ice Age showed a huge land connecting Asia and Americas.			

TIP Look for words that show present (is, can, has), past (were) and future (would) settings.

F **Look at the highlighted words in the passage. Find out what they mean using the Mini-dictionary on pages 69–72.**

Integration

 16 **Read the paragraph. Write details that show *Present* and *Future*.**

> I think building the Intercontinental Peace Bridge is impossible. Just think of the icebergs in the Bering Strait. The icebergs would just destroy the bridge pillars. Also, there are no roads or railways in Alaska or Siberia that go all the way to the coasts—thousands of kilometers of new roads and railway tracks would have to be built.

Present	Future
1 _____	1 _____
_____	_____
2 _____	2 _____
_____	_____

H **17** **Listen and complete the paragraph.**

I think we can build the **(1)** _____

Peace Bridge. If the bridge pillars are very **(2)** _____

and shaped like ice-breaking **(3)** _____, they could

(4) _____ icebergs. Russia has already made railways

that are almost **(5)** _____ long. So it is possible to make

railways that are **(6)** _____ enough to reach the coasts.

I **Work with a classmate. On a separate piece of paper, design a bridge that connects Asia and the Americas. Then present it to the class.**

A What are your favorite tourist spots? Discuss your answers.

Reading Skill

Understanding brochures

A brochure is a thin book that gives information about a product or a service. Well-planned brochures can make you want to buy something.

B Label the parts of the brochure. Write the letter.

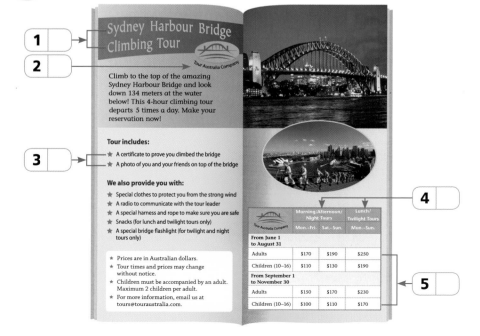

Sydney Harbour Bridge Climbing Tour

Tour Australia Company

Climb to the top of the amazing Sydney Harbour Bridge and look down 134 meters at the water below! This 4-hour climbing tour departs 5 times a day. Make your reservation now!

Tour includes:
★ A certificate to prove you climbed the bridge
★ A photo of you and your friends on top of the bridge

We also provide you with:
★ Special clothes to protect you from the strong wind
★ A radio to communicate with the tour leader
★ A special harness and rope to make sure you are safe
★ Snacks (for lunch and twilight tours only)
★ A special bridge flashlight (for twilight and night tours only)

★ Prices are in Australian dollars.
★ Tour times and prices may change without notice.
★ Children must be accompanied by an adult. Maximum 2 children per adult.
★ For more information, email us at tours@touraustralia.com.

	Morning/Afternoon/ Night Tours		Lunch/ Twilight Tours
	Mon.-Fri.	Sat.-Sun.	Mon.-Sun.
From June 1 to August 31			
Adults	$170	$190	$250
Children (10–16)	$110	$130	$190
From September 1 to November 30			
Adults	$150	$170	$230
Children (10–16)	$100	$110	$170

A name of tour

B cost of tour

C tours offered

D what you get after the tour

E name of the tour company

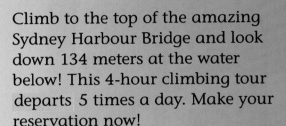
Sydney Harbour Bridge Climbing Tour

Tour Australia Company

Climb to the top of the amazing Sydney Harbour Bridge and look down 134 meters at the water below! This 4-hour climbing tour departs 5 times a day. Make your reservation now!

Tour includes:

★ A certificate to prove you climbed the bridge

★ A photo of you and your friends on top of the bridge

We also provide you with:

★ Special clothes to protect you from the strong wind

★ A radio to communicate with the tour leader

★ A special harness and rope to make sure you are safe

★ Snacks (for lunch and twilight tours only)

★ A special bridge flashlight (for twilight and night tours only)

★ Prices are in Australian dollars.

★ Tour times and prices may change without notice.

★ Children must be accompanied by an adult. Maximum 2 children per adult.

★ For more information, email us at tours@touraustralia.com.

Tour Australia Company	Morning/Afternoon/ Night Tours		Lunch/ Twilight Tours
	Mon.–Fri.	Sat.–Sun.	Mon.–Sun.
From June 1 to August 31			
Adults	$170	$190	$250
Children (10–16)	$110	$130	$190
From September 1 to November 30			
Adults	$150	$170	$230
Children (10–16)	$100	$110	$170

Practice

D Write the answers.

1 What kind of tour does the brochure advertise? _____

2 How much does it cost for a 12-year-old child to take a twilight tour in August?

_____

3 How many tours are offered every day? _____

4 How long does the tour last? _____

5 How high above the water does the tour take people? _____

6 What does the tour include? _____

7 What are provided to ensure safety on the tours?

_____

8 What is not provided for the night tour? _____

9 How much would it cost for one adult and two children to take an afternoon tour on a

Sunday in November? _____

10 Can children go on the tour by themselves? _____

11 Why does a person get a certificate after the tour? _____

_____

12 In which months are the prices lower? _____

TIP Write notes on the brochure to help you find and remember the information easily. Write things like "prices" and "dates."

E Look at the highlighted words in the brochure. Find out what they mean using the Mini-dictionary on pages 69–72.

Integration

F Read the notes about the Sydney Harbour Bridge climbing tour. Then write out some of the notes as questions.

- children aged 9?
- Tour guides / languages?
- certificates / look like?

- older sister / 17?
- special shoes?
- if it rains?

- $ / 1 Sep to 30 Nov. / why?
- digital camera / allowed?
- camcorder / safe?

1   Can children aged 9 take the tour?

2

3

4

5

6

G On a separate piece of paper, write a letter to the tour company asking the questions above. Then read your letter to the class.

(19) **Read the brochure.**

Take the Millau Viaduct bicycle tour!

Feel what it's like to fly like a bird above the morning clouds …

We provide the bicycle, protective gear and a guide who will tell you all about the bridge.

Saturdays, Sundays and public holidays only.

Prices:
Adults: 15 Euros
Children (9–15): 12 Euros

Note: Children must be accompanied by an adult.

The History of the Millau Viaduct

In 1989, the French government was looking for a way to solve the traffic problem in the Tarn Valley. Officials wanted to build a new bridge to stop the cars from getting stuck in the valley. But they were worried about building something that might destroy the scenery or upset the people who lived in the valley.

In December 2004, the Millau Viaduct opened. The bridge is so beautiful that it almost looks like a natural part of the valley. With some parts of the bridge taller than the Eiffel Tower, tourists (numbering 10,000–25,000 every day) can drive on the bridge and feel like they are flying over the valley. Below the bridge, the valley's people are enjoying life with fewer cars and less pollution.

B **Write a sentence from the brochure that shows mood.**

_____

_____

C **Write the answers.**

1 What kind of tour does the brochure advertise?

_____

2 How much would it cost for one adult and two children to take the tour?

_____

3 On which days can you take the tour?

_____

4 What does the tour company provide?

_____

5 Can two children, aged seven and 10, take the tour together? Why or why not?

_____

_____

D **Look at the history of the Millau Viaduct. Circle the correct setting. Then check the details that show the setting.**

Paragraph 1

Setting: past / present / future

1 1989 ☐

2 traffic problem ☐

3 beautiful bridge ☐

4 2004 ☐

Paragraph 2

Setting: past / present /future

1 destroying the scenery ☐

2 driving on the bridge ☐

3 opening of the bridge ☐

4 less pollution ☐

A **What sports are played at the Olympic Games? Discuss your answers.**

Reading Skill

Understanding summaries

A summary states the main ideas in just a few sentences. Good summaries use simple words and short sentences.

B **Check [✓] two sentences that summarize the paragraph.**

The Olympic Games are the world's oldest multi-sporting event. They started in 776 B.C. in a place called Olympia in Greece. The games stopped in A.D. 393. They were started again by a Frenchman named Pierre de Coubertin in 1896.

1 The Olympic Games started in 776 B.C. in Greece. ☐

2 The ancient Olympic Games were held every four years. ☐

3 The games stopped in A.D. 393 but started again in 1896. ☐

The History of the Olympic Games

The Olympic Games are the world's oldest multisporting event. They started in 776 B.C. in a place called Olympia in Greece. The games stopped in A.D. 393, but started again in 1896.

The Ancient Olympics

According to stories, King Ifitos of Elis in Greece started the games as a way to stop the fighting among Greek kingdoms. Instead of fighting, the warriors competed in sporting events. There were about 20 events and only Greek men could join. It cost a lot of money to train for and travel to the games. Winners received a crown of olive leaves and often had poems written or statues made in their honor.

The Modern Olympics

A Frenchman named Pierre de Coubertin organized the first modern Olympic Games. He wanted to promote sports and thought it would be better for young men to compete

than fight. The first games were held in Athens in 1896 and had 245 participants from 15 nations. At the time it was the biggest international sporting event. The recent games in Athens involved 11,100 participants from 202 countries.

The modern Olympic Games are held every four years. These are divided into the Summer and Winter Games, which are held two years apart. Winners get a gold, silver or bronze medal.

D Answer the questions.

1 When did the ancient Olympic Games stop?

2 Who could compete in the ancient Olympic Games?

3 How many nations competed at the recent Olympic Games in Athens?

E Check [✓] two sentences that summarize each paragraph.

Paragraph 2

1 Warriors competed in sporting events.

2 The ancient Olympic Games were meant to stop the fighting among Greek kingdoms.

3 Winners were made famous through poems or statues.

4 King Ifitos of Elis in Greece started the games.

Paragraph 3

1 The modern Olympic Games were started in 1896 by Pierre de Coubertin.

2 The first games were held in Athens.

3 The modern Olympic Games have grown hugely in the number of participants.

4 Pierre de Coubertin wanted to promote sports.

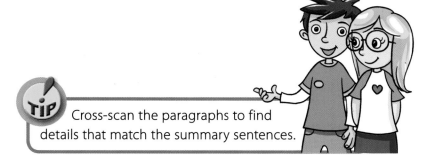

TiP Cross-scan the paragraphs to find details that match the summary sentences.

  F Look at the highlighted words in the passage. Find out what these words mean using the Mini-dictionary on pages 69–72.

G 🎧 **21** **Read the dialogue about the Olympic Games. Then write a summary of each paragraph.**

> I think the Olympic Games are a good thing. They get people from different nations to compete in a way that's fun and not dangerous. This encourages people to share ideas. This way, they can learn to understand one another better.

_____

_____

_____

_____

> I don't think the Olympic Games are important. I don't see how we can better understand people of other cultures when we're competing with them—we would be too busy thinking about winning. I think it's easier to learn about other cultures through real friendships than through "friendly" competitions. Through friendships, we learn to respect our differences.

_____

_____

_____

_____

H **What do you think is good about the Olympic Games? Tell the class.**

A Who is your favorite Olympic champion? Discuss your answer.

Reading Skill

Identifying character

Character is what a person is like. Is the person brave, weak, smart or silly? Knowing people's character helps you better understand the passage and predict what might happen next.

B Check [✓] the words/phrases that best describe the person in the paragraph.

Meet the young lady who is not afraid to throw herself over tall things! Yelena Isinbayeva won the Women's Pole Vault event in the 2004 Olympic Games in Athens, setting a new world record of 4.91 meters. But that was not enough for Yelena. The following year, at the World Championships in Finland, she cleared a height of 5.01 meters, making her the first woman to jump over 5 meters!

brave ☐

happy ☐

likes to compete ☐

likes to improve ☐

▶ p r o f i l e

Yelena Isinbayeva
Queen of the Leap

Meet the young lady who is not afraid to throw herself over tall things! Yelena Isinbayeva won the Women's Pole Vault event in the 2004 Olympic Games in Athens, setting a new world record of 4.91 meters. But that was not enough for Yelena. The following year, at the World Championships in Finland, she cleared a height of 5.01 meters, making her the first woman to jump over 5 meters!

Yelena was born in Russia on June 3, 1982. She started out doing gymnastics when she was five years old. However, by the time she was 15 she was too tall and was encouraged to try pole vaulting instead. Her gymnastics training helped her in this new event. Soon, she was breaking world records.

Yelena is very close to her family. One time, her parents banned her from driving because they were worried that she might get hurt. She rode the streetcar instead! She still lives with her parents and younger sister in her hometown of Volgograd. When she is not training, she likes to help her mother in the kitchen.

Yelena has a Bachelor's degree. Believe it or not, she is also a member of the Russian army and holds the rank of Senior Lieutenant. She dreams of opening a restaurant someday.

 **Answer the questions.**

1 How old is Yelena now?

2 What did Yelena achieve at the 2004 Olympic Games?

3 Why did Yelena's parents ban her from driving?

 Write details from the article that support the descriptions.

Yelena's character	Supporting details
1 willing to try new things	
2 thinks about her future	
3 loves her family	
4 likes cooking	
5 values education	
6 likes discipline	

Tip Scan the article for details that support the descriptions.

F **Look at the highlighted words in the article. Find out what they mean using the Mini-dictionary on pages 69–72.**

23 Read about Shizuka Arakawa. Then check [✓] the questions that show interesting things about her character.

Name: Shizuka Arakawa

Date of birth: December 29, 1981

Place of birth: Sendai, Japan

Height: 166 cm

Famous for:
- Winning Japan's first ever Olympic gold medal in figure-skating, at the 2006 Winter Olympic Games in Turin, Italy
- Being the first female skater born in Asia to win an Olympic gold medal in figure skating

1   When did you decide to become a figure skater?

2   How long did it take you to become good at figure skating?

3   What is your favorite city?

4   How many hours a day do you train?

5   Who is your best friend?

6   What do you like to do in your free time?

H Think of an athlete who you would like to interview. Write questions that will show his/her character. Then tell the class.

1 _____

2 _____

3 _____

4 _____

5 _____

6 _____

A 24 **Read the passage.**

Milo of Croton

Throughout the history of the Olympic Games there have been many famous champions. But one of the most famous and successful Olympians was also one of the most ancient. From a place in southern Italy called Croton came a strong man named Milo. Milo won the wrestling event five times. That means he was the champion for more than 20 years!

Milo competed at the 60th Olympic Games and won the Boys' Wrestling event. At the 62nd through the 66th Olympics (532–516 B.C.), he won the Men's Wrestling event. When he competed at the 67th Olympics in 512 B.C., he was defeated by a younger man. At that time, Milo must have been at least 40 years old, or perhaps even older.

Milo's strength was very famous. He trained by carrying a cow on his back up a mountain. He enjoyed showing off his strength as well. Sometimes he would hold out one hand and challenge someone to move his fingers. No one could move even his smallest finger.

However, Milo was not just a wrestler. He led the army of Croton to many victories. He was also a student of the famous Pythagoras and enjoyed poetry and art. In one legend, he protected his friends by holding up the roof when the building was falling down. He did not let go until all of his friends had gotten out safely.

B **Check [✓] two sentences that summarize each paragraph.**

Paragraph 1

1   The Olympic Games and Milo of Croton are ancient.   ☐

2   Milo was one of the most famous Olympic athletes.   ☐

3   Milo was the Olympic wrestling champion for more than 20 years.   ☐

4   There have been many famous Olympic champions.   ☐

Paragraph 2

1   Milo competed in seven Olympic Games, once as a boy, six times as an adult.   ☐

2   Milo won the Boy's Wrestling event.   ☐

3   Milo competed in five Olympic Games, but did not win every time.   ☐

4   Milo was quite old when he competed at his last Olympic Games.   ☐

C **Write details from the passage that support the descriptions.**

Milo's character	Supporting details
1 determined to win every time	
2 enjoyed competing at a young age	
3 loyal to friends	
4 liked attention	

Historic Cities

A What do you know about your city's history? Discuss your answers.

Reading Skill

Understanding paragraph development

Passages are developed using well-ordered paragraphs. Knowing how paragraphs are built helps you better understand a reading.

B Number the sentences in the correct order.

☐ **A** When adults played, it was quite dangerous. ☐ **B** They had courts for ceremonial ball games. ☐ **C** Children played a safer version for fun. ☐ **D** The Maya also knew how to have fun.

C ♪ 25 **Read the passage.**

The Mighty Maya

The Maya in central America is one of the world's most well-known ancient civilizations. Its classical period lasted between the years A.D. 250 and 900. Ⓐ

Though far from Europe, the Maya civilization had a lot in common with Greece and Egypt. Ⓑ Just like the Greeks, the Maya had stone buildings and they worshipped gods. They also had many independent city-states similar to those of ancient Greece. Like the Egyptians, the Maya built very tall pyramids. Ⓒ

The Maya achieved a lot of things that were unique to their civilization. Some of their cities were very large. The city of Tikal had 100,000 to 200,000 people. Ⓓ The Maya also invented things like rubber balls and shoes. Ⓔ They were very good at mathematics and astronomy.

The Maya also knew how to have fun. They had courts for ceremonial ball games. Ⓕ When adults played, it was quite dangerous. Ⓖ Children played a safer version for fun.

Ⓗ The Maya civilization started to decline after A.D. 900, but we can still visit their old sites and cities. Even after thousands of years, the Maya achievements are still impressive.

D Answer the questions.

1 How long did the Maya classical period last?

2 How were the Maya similar to the Egyptians?

3 What did the Maya invent?

Practice

E Insert each sentence into the passage. Write the letter.

1 Some of the similarities between these civilizations were quite amazing. **B**

2 They were quite good thinkers.

3 Almost every Maya city had at least one of these ball courts.

4 This was a period of more than 600 years.

5 The Maya pyramids had temple rooms at the top, but had the same steep sides and steps as the Egyptian ones.

6 Of course, even great civilizations start to break down as time goes by.

7 That is as big as some of today's modern cities.

8 Pictures show adult players bleeding from injuries.

TIP When you come to a circled letter in the passage, scan the sentences above and decide which sentence builds on the information given in the passage.

F Look at the highlighted words in the passage. Find out what they mean using the Mini-dictionary on pages 69–72.

Integration

G 🎧 **26** **Listen and complete the paragraph.**

The ancient Maya **(1)**_____ ball games not just for fun
but as a religious activity. The ball games were played in
(2)_____ of different sizes, with some sized 166 meters
long and 68 meters **(3)**_____. **A** At either
end of the court, there was a stone
ring on the wall. The players passed
a large rubber ball through the
ring to score a goal. **B** The game
was **(4)**_____ because
of the stone walls and players
hitting each other. **C** However, losing
the **(5)**_____ was even more
dangerous! **D**

H **Insert each sentence into the paragraph above. Write the letter.**

1 The first team to do this was the winner. ☐

2 Sometimes, the losing team was killed as a sacrifice to the gods. ☐

3 The courts were shaped like a capital "I" and had stone walls and ramps. ☐

4 For this reason, players wore special padding to protect themselves. ☐

I **What is your favorite ball game? Tell the class.**

A What would you do if you got lost in a new place? Discuss your answers.

Reading Skill

Understanding signs

Signs help you in many different ways. They give directions, rules, or information on places, events, prices and times.

B What information do these signs give? Write your answers.

1

Jay's Souvenir Store
100 meters

2

_____

_____

C ►27 **Read about Chichen Itza and look at the signs.**

Chichen Itza is one of the most famous Maya cities that can still be seen and explored today. The ruins of this once great city include houses, temples, palaces and ball courts. Here are some of the signs you'll find around the Chichen Itza site.

A

Souvenir Store
100 meters

B

El Caracol Observatory
Maya astronomers observed the Sun, moon and stars from this building.

C

Please put all litter in the trash cans.

D

↑ Temple of Kukulcan
← Great Ball Court   Observatory →

E

Guided tours leave from here. Please buy tickets at the main gate.

F

Temple of the Warriors
Pyramid with warrior statues of ston.

G

Parking
← Tour Buses   Private Cars →

H

← Traditional Maya food
Kiosk for snacks and drinks →

I

Admission
Adults: $24
Children (under 12): $10
Open Monday to Sunday,
9.00 a.m.–5.30 p.m.

J

Temple of Kukulcan (El Castillo)
This well-preserved temple is on top of an older pyramid, where you can see the Jaguar Throne.

D Answer the questions.

1 Which sign tells us where we can buy food?

2 What time does the Chichen Itza site close?

3 What are the warrior statues made of?

E Choose the correct sign for each statement. Write the letter.

1 Buses park to the left, cars park to the right. ⓖ

2 Turn left if you want to eat Maya food. Turn right for snacks and drinks. ◯

3 Do not leave trash on the ground. ◯

4 Go there if you want to buy something to remember your trip by. ◯

5 It is an old building built on top of an older building. ◯

6 This is how much it costs to get in. ◯

7 These are the directions to three famous places in the site. ◯

8 It is a building for soldiers. ◯

9 This unique building was where the Maya people watched the sky. ◯

10 Buy your tickets first and then meet here to start the tour. ◯

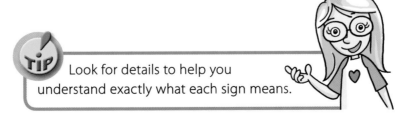

Tip   Look for details to help you understand exactly what each sign means.

 Look at the highlighted words in the reading. Find out what they mean using the Mini-dictionary on pages 69–72.

Integration

Read the signs. What information do they give? Write the number.

| 1 rules | 2 directions to places | 3 prices or times | 4 special places or things |

A
Airport Buses →
50 meters

C
Anna's Diner
The best burger place in town

B
Please do not write on the walls.

D
Bicycle Shed
Open 8.00 a.m.–4.00 p.m.

H **Make your own signs. Then present them to the class.**

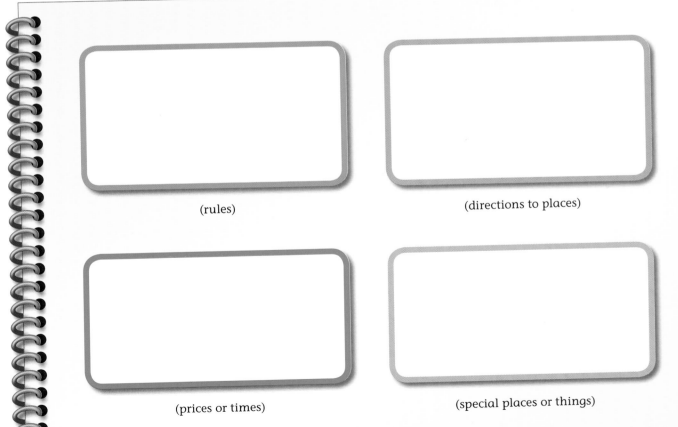

(rules)

(directions to places)

(prices or times)

(special places or things)

 Read the passage.

The Maya Society

Kings were very important to the Maya. Without a king, kingdoms would fall and disappear. The greater a king was, the more people came to live in his city. **A**

The Maya were very good artists. The art that they made on pottery, stones and temple walls is often said to be the most beautiful in ancient America.

B The writing system of the Maya is one of the oldest in the Americas. At present, there are almost 10,000 examples of Maya writing. The Maya wrote on walls, pottery, monuments and even tree bark. They used red and black ink in a lot of their writing. **C**

B Check [✓] two sentences that summarize the third paragraph.

1 There are thousands of examples of ancient Maya writing.

2 The ancient Maya liked to write on tree barks.

3 Ancient Maya writing was found on monuments.

4 The Maya wrote on anything, using a lot of red and black ink.

C Insert each sentence into the passage above. Write the letter.

1 This caused neighboring kingdoms to call the Maya cities the "land of black and red."

2 The importance of kings makes the Maya civilization similar to many other civilizations.

3 Another interesting thing about the Maya was their writing.

 30 **Read the signs. Then choose the correct sign for each statement. Write the letter.**

A

Jail
This strong stone building had wooden bars across the windows and doors.

C

Guided Tours
2 hours: $12
Half day: $18
Full day: $24

B

↑
Exit
← Information   Kiosk →

D

Do not climb the sides of the pyramid

1 A tour guide can show you around the site for a few hours, half a day or the whole day. ☐

2 Walking on the pyramid can be dangerous, so please do not do that. ☐

3 Go straight ahead if you want to leave. Turn right if you want drinks or snacks. Turn left if you want to ask for information. ☐

4 It is a place for people who did bad things. ☐

E **Which signs give the following information? Write the letter.**

1 directions to places ☐   **3** special places or things ☐

2 rules ☐   **4** prices or times ☐

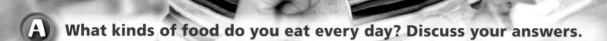

A **What kinds of food do you eat every day? Discuss your answers.**

Reading Skill

Finding information from graphs

Like tables, graphs show you detailed information quickly and clearly.

B **Identify the information in the graph. Write the letter.**

A the minimum (smallest) amount of vegetables we should eat daily

B the maximum (largest) amount of grain we should eat daily

C the food we should eat more of

D the minimum amount of grain we should eat daily

E the maximum amount of vegetables we should eat daily

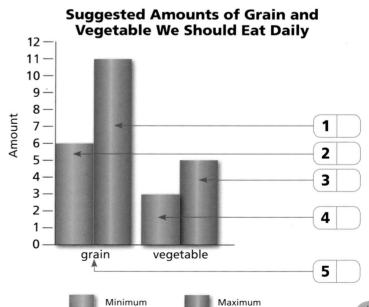

Suggested Amounts of Grain and Vegetable We Should Eat Daily

1
2
3
4
5

Minimum   Maximum

How to Eat Healthy

Food is a basic part of living and growing. It gives your body the energy it needs to work. It also gives your body important nutrients— the things that help your body grow and become stronger. You need different kinds of nutrients, such as carbohydrates, fats, vitamins, minerals and proteins.

Your body gets carbohydrates from foods like cereal, bread, pasta, rice, fruit and vegetables. Your body gets fats from margarine, butter and sweets. Vitamins and minerals can be found in foods like eggs, meat, nuts, soy beans, bananas or even table salt. Proteins are found in dairy products like milk, cheese and yogurt but also in meat, fish, eggs and beans.

However, you do not need all the nutrients in the same amounts. Your body needs a lot of carbohydrates but not too much fat. To have a balanced diet, it will be useful to find out how many servings of each food you need every day.

What counts as one serving?

Grain
- 1 slice of bread
- 1 ounce of cereal
- ½ cup of cooked cereal, rice or pasta

Vegetable
- 1 cup of raw leafy vegetables
- ½ cup of other vegetables—cooked or chopped raw
- ¾ cup of vegetable juice

Fruit
- 1 medium apple, banana or orange
- ½ cup of chopped, cooked or canned fruit
- ¾ cup of fruit juice

Dairy
- 1 cup of milk or yogurt
- 1 ½ ounces of natural cheese
- 2 ounces of processed cheese

Meat, fish and egg
- 2–3 ounces of cooked lean meat, poultry or fish
- ½ cup of cooked dry beans or 1 egg counts as 1 ounce of lean meat.
- 2 tablespoons of peanut butter or ⅓ cup of nuts counts as 1 ounce of meat.

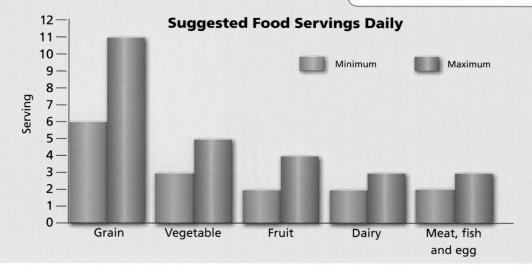

Suggested Food Servings Daily

60

D Answer the questions.

1 What are nutrients?

2 What are examples of dairy products?

3 Which do we need more of, carbohydrates or fats?

E Look at the graph and write the answers.

1 Which color on the graph shows the maximum food servings? _____

2 What is the minimum serving of fruit we should have every day? _____

3 What is the maximum serving of dairy products we should have every day? _____

4 Would eight servings of cereal, rice or pasta every day be OK? _____

5 Add the minimum servings of fruit and vegetables. How many servings are there altogether? _____

6 Which should we eat more of, meat or vegetables? _____

TIP Use the numbers and different colors on the graph to guide you to the information you need.

F Look at the highlighted words in the passage. Find out what they mean using the Mini-dictionary on pages 69–72.

Integration

G Write what you and three classmates usually eat.

Name	Breakfast	Lunch	Dinner
1 Me			
2			
3			
4			

H Make a graph for one of your classmates using the information above. Then present it to the class.

Student's name: _____

Serving

12 —
11 —
10 —
9 —
8 —
7 —
6 —
5 —
4 —
3 —
2 —
1 —
0 —

Grain   Vegetable   Fruit   Dairy   Meat, fish and egg

Out at the Diner

A What do you usually order when eating out? Discuss your answers.

Reading Skill

Understanding menus

A menu lists the different foods and drinks that are available in a restaurant. It tells you what they are made from, how much they cost and how big the servings are.

B Check [✓] the information you can identify.

Tony's Diner
It's good for you!

Breakfast (all day from 6:00 a.m.)	Regular	Large
White Rice with Mixed Vegetables *	$2.89	$4.49
With or without egg topping		
Granola Cereal with Fresh Fruit	$1.89	$3.49
With or without milk		
Fruit Smoothie *	$1.49	$2.49
Papaya, strawberry or celery		

Note: Items marked * can be delivered between 3:00 p.m. and 9:00 p.m. daily, but only as large orders.

meals offered ☐

time that drinks are served ☐

meal servings ☐

prices ☐

delivery service ☐

C ◌○32 **Read the menu.**

Tony's Diner
It's good for you!

	Regular	Large
Breakfast (all day from 6:00 a.m.)		
White Rice with Mixed Vegetables *	$2.89	$4.49
With or without egg topping		
Granola Cereal with Fresh Fruit ····	$1.89	$3.49
With or without milk		
Fruit Smoothie * ···	$1.49	$2.49
Papaya, strawberry or celery		
Lunch (from 11:30 a.m.)		
Sandwich on a Stick *	$4.25	$7.45
Whole grain bread with vegetable and meat		
Pasta Perfect ········	$5.25	$8.45
Pasta with wild mushrooms		
Fruit Salad ········	$4.25	$7.35
A platter of seven different fruits		
Dinner (from 5:30 p.m.)		
Veggie Burger ········	$3.29	$4.59
Grilled vegetable burger on a bun		
Stuffed Bread * ········	$3.45	$5.49
Bread with chicken and avocado filling		
Steak Surprise ········	$5.75	$9.85
Grilled steak with vegetable and baked potato		
Juice (orange, apple, grape, lime, watermelon)	$1.99	

Note: Items marked * can be delivered between 3:00 p.m. and 9:00 p.m. daily, but only as large orders.

D Answer the questions.

1 How much does a large order of granola cereal cost? $3.49

2 What is in the Stuffed Bread? chiken and avocado

3 How many meals are available for delivery? 2.

Practice

E Write the name of the meal and the serving size for each person.

1 It is 2:00 p.m. Frank likes bread. He is hungry and he can eat a lot.

   Sandwich on a Stick, large

2 It is 7:00 a.m. Rebecca wants something with egg, but she is not very hungry.

   White Rice with Raised Vegetables.   Regular.

3 It is 7:30 a.m. Thomas really likes fruit but he does not like milk. He is very hungry.

   Fruit Smoothie.   Large.

4 It is 8:00 p.m. Karly really likes steak but she is not very hungry.

   Steak Surprise.   Regular

5 It is 5:00 p.m. Peter is very hungry. He wants to eat something with mushrooms.

   Pasta Perfect   Large.

TIP Note the time of day and how hungry the person is.

F Look at the highlighted words in the menu. Find out what they mean using the Mini-dictionary on pages 69–72.

Integration

G Write a healthy menu for a new diner.

_____
(name of diner)

	Regular	Large
Breakfast (from _____ to _____)		
• _____ _____	$_____	$_____
• _____ _____	$_____	$_____
Lunch (from _____ to _____)		
• _____ _____	$_____	$_____
• _____ _____	$_____	$_____
Dinner (from _____)		
• _____ _____	$_____	$_____
• _____ _____	$_____	$_____

Drinks

• _____ $_____   • _____ $_____

• _____ $_____   • _____ $_____

 H Exchange menus with a classmate. Ask and answer.

What would you like?

I would like a large order of spaghetti and an apple juice, please.

A  Read the passage.

Going Easy on Snacks and Fast Food

Fats are common in the food we eat. In the right amount, they are good for us. **A** They give us energy and protect our bodies from cold weather. However, not all kinds of fats are good for us. **B** One unhealthy kind of fat is called trans fat. Trans fat can cause serious heart problems, but it is used in many foods because it helps the food keep its flavor longer. Trans fats are common in snacks or fast food. **C** If we eat a lot of these foods, we are putting our health in danger.

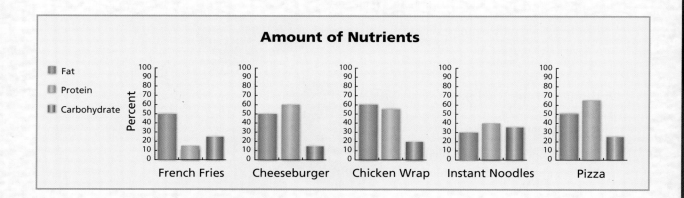

Amount of Nutrients

Legend: Fat, Protein, Carbohydrate

French Fries · Cheeseburger · Chicken Wrap · Instant Noodles · Pizza

B Insert the sentence into the paragraph above. Write the letter.

Snacks and fast food are often high in fat and we need to be careful how much of these foods we eat every day.

C Look at the graph and write the answers.

1 What color shows fat content? _____

2 How much protein does a cheeseburger have? _____

3 What do the graphs show about the fat content in snacks and fast food?

_____

D 🎧 34 **Read the menu.**

Helen's Heaven

Lunch (from 11:00 a.m.)

	Regular	Large
Seafood Pasta Spaghetti with mussels and tomato sauce	$4.25	$7.45
Yellow and Green Salad Fresh lettuce with orange slices	$3.25	$6.35

Dinner (from 5:30 p.m.)

	Regular	Large
Salmon Plate Smoked salmon with mushrooms, lettuce, string beans and tomatoes	$5.25	$7.45
Beef Roast Roasted beef with grilled red onions and avocado	$5.99	$8.25

E **Write the name of the meal and the serving size for each of your friends.**

1 It is 7:00 p.m. Your friend likes beef. She is not very hungry.

Beef Roast.   Regular

2 It is 11:30 a.m. Your friend loves spaghetti and he is very hungry.

Seafood Pasta   Large.

Mini-dictionary

A

(ə kʌmpeni) 陪伴

accompany	v	to go with another person or other people	p. 34
admission	n	the price to go into a building or participate in an event	p. 54
amazing	adj	surprising; fantastic	p. 14
argue	v	to give reasons for or against	p. 24
asteroid	n	any of the large objects between Mars and Jupiter	p. 24
astronomer	n	a scientist who studies space, stars and planets	p. 24
astronomy	n	the study of space, stars and planets	p. 50
attempt	n	tries; acts of trying	p. 20

B

bachelor's degree	n	a qualification given to a person who has finished university	p. 44
balanced diet	n	regular eating of the right foods in the right amount	p. 60
ban	v	to say that something must not be done	p. 44
bronze	adj	a kind of red-brown metal	p. 40

C

carbohydrate	n	food (usually made from plants) with carbon, hydrogen or oxygen	p. 60
ceremonial	adj	part of a special event	p. 50
certificate	n	a special document showing something is true or has been done	p. 34
chatter	v	to talk fast without stopping, especially about unimportant things	p. 14
civilization	n	a society that is well-organized and developed	p. 50
classical period	n	time of great art and success	p. 50
classify	v	to put in a special group	p. 24
clear	v	to jump over something without touching it	p. 44
communicate	v	to talk or send messages	p. 34
compete	v	to take part in a contest	p. 40
complete	adj	having all the necessary parts; whole; full	p. 10
condition	n	the state that something is in	p. 20
continent	n	a large area of land surrounded by sea	p. 30
criteria	n	standards on which a decision may be based	p. 24
crown	n	something circular and decorative worn on the head to show victory or honor	p. 40
culture	n	the way people live and their beliefs	p. 30

D

decline	v	to go down in level or importance; to become smaller or weaker	p. 50
demand	v	to ask for or command strongly	p. 14

depart	v	to leave	p. 34
disappear	v	to become impossible to see or find; to vanish	p. 10
disaster	n	a sudden bad end or failure	p. 20
discovery	n	the act of finding	p. 24
distant	adj	far away; not close	p. 24
dwarf	adj	smaller than the normal size	p. 24

E

echo	v	to make a sound that repeats	p. 14
encourage	v	to say or do something that helps someone take action	p. 44
energy	n	the power or strength to do work	p. 60
exist	v	to be: to be real	p. 20
explore	v	to travel through or look at something carefully to find out what is there or what it is like	p. 20

F

| filling | n | a food mixture that is put inside a pie, sandwich or other types of food | p. 64 |

G

gasp	v	to make a quick breathing sound	p. 14
granola cereal	n	breakfast food made from grains, fruits and nuts	p. 64
grilled	adj	cooked over direct heat, using a grill	p. 64
guided tour	n	a trip led by someone who tells interesting information about the place	p. 54
gymnastics	n	a sport in which a person does exercises on metal bars to show strength, balance and body control	p. 44

H

| harbour (british english) harbor (american english) | n | water along the coast where ships can go safely | p. 34 |
| harness | n | strong material that is put around a person to stop them from falling | p. 34 |

I

icy	adj	very cold	p. 24
impossible	adj	not possible; cannot be done	p. 10
impressive	adj	amazing; admirable	p. 50
include	v	to have; to contain; to be part of	p. 34
independent	adj	not ruled or controlled by others	p. 50
intercontinental	adj	going from one continent to another	p. 30
international date line	n	an invisible line that separates each calendar day from the next (the date to the east of the line is one day later than the west)	p. 30
involve	v	to include; to have	p. 40

K

| kingdom | n | a country with a king or queen as the ruler | p. 40 |
| kiosk | n | a small structure, with one or more open sides, that is used for selling things | p. 54 |

restore	v	to bring or put something back to the way it was before	p. 10
ruin	n	the part of a building that is left after the rest has been destroyed	p. 54

S

separate	v	to keep apart; to make a distance between	p. 30
serving	n	an amount of food eaten at one time	p. 60
smoothie	n	a creamy drink made of fruit or vegetable blended with juice, milk or yogurt	p. 64
snap	v	to make a short sharp sound	p. 10
souvenir	adj	for or relating to a souvenir—something that a person keeps to remember a place	p. 54
soy bean	n	seed of an Asian plant from which oil and food are made	p. 60
stare	v	to look hard and long	p. 14
statue	n	a stone or metal decoration made to look like a person	p. 40
steak	n	a large thick piece of meat, usually beef	p. 64
strait	n	a narrow passage of water that connects larger seas	p. 30
streetcar	n	a vehicle (like a small train) that moves on rails and carries passengers	p. 44
successful	adj	having the intended effect or result	p. 20
surface	n	the top or outside layer	p. 20
sweets	n	foods containing a lot of sugar	p. 60

T

temple	n	a special building where people worship gods	p. 54
throne	n	a special chair for a king or queen	p. 54
topping	n	food put on top of another food to make it look nicer or taste better	p. 64
trade	n	the business of buying and selling	p. 30
twilight	adj	relating to the the time when day is starting to become night	p. 34

U

unique	adj	special; one of a kind	p. 50
usable	adj	can work and be used	p. 30

V

vitamin	n	natural substance important for good health	p. 60

W

wand	n	a small stick used for doing magic tricks	p. 10
whole grain bread	n	bread that uses all of the grain, including the outer layer	p. 64
wink	v	to close and open one eye very quickly	p. 14
withstand	v	to resist or stand against; to stay strong or unharmed	p. 30
world record	n	the best performance or achievement in the world	p. 44
worried	adj	uneasy or troubled about something	p. 44
worship	v	to show respect and love for a god by praying	p. 50